To JACK —
a new friend!
Best wishes —
Barbara Nixon H...
11/28/08
Lewisburg, WV

200

THE FURTIVE WALL

THE FURTIVE WALL

POEMS BY
DANIEL HABERMAN

ETCHINGS BY
JAN STUSSY

NEW YORK
ART DIRECTION BOOK COMPANY
1982

Art Direction Book Company,
10 East 39 Street, New York City 10016

NO PART OF THIS BOOK MAY BE REPRODUCED,
OR TRANSMITTED IN A RETRIEVAL SYSTEM,
OR TRANSMITTED IN ANY FORM OR BY ANY MEANS,
ELECTRONIC, MECHANICAL, PHOTOCOPYING, RECORDING OR OTHERWISE
WITHOUT THE PRIOR PERMISSION OF THE PUBLISHERS.

All rights reserved
Library of Congress catalog card number: 81-69556
ISBN: 0-910158-84-3
Copyright © 1982 by Daniel Haberman

Printed in the United States of America

for Barbara

NOTE

Acknowledgments are due to the following publications, in which some of these poems have appeared:

Broadway
New York Quarterly
Pulp
Sun & Moon

The translations of Archilochus, Erinna, Praxilla, Gaetulicus, Zenobius and Antipater of Sidon were done in collaboration with Marylin B. Arthur.

CONTENTS

And he who can weep can hope . . . for the blood
around the heart is the thought of men

Lev Shestov & Empedocles

There is a wall—a furtive wall
Bluely dark in among the hills:
Come rest your thought
Leave behind the wills,
Then go beyond
Bring your human ills.
I signal now a poising call
There beyond the furtive wall . . .

Even now the russet winds blow
Over and over the lanky field;
Long, since the banking geese heel
And the tiny snows stray
Into and out a promenade of trees
While grass receives
The whitened shame,
Acquiesced into the violet same . . .

Red Hand of the Sun high above the wood
Winters slow into the windfall night:
    I have seen a possum quail
    Talking to the nightingale,
Winters slow into the windfall night;
    I have seen a quiet thrush
    Leaping to the barren brush,
Winters slow into the windfall night;
    Would there be a fluted bird
    Howling beauty's darker word,
Red Hand of the Sun high above the wood
Winters slow into the windfall night . . .

The trees in gentle umbrage swayed,
Determined Time's no perch to loiter,
The dancing fears were unallayed,
The soul was weary of the slaughter;

Dreams were real — the real were dreams
And all beside I might have seen:
The heart won't mistress to the mind,
My heart's not mistress to my mind.

THE WAY OF IT

With the futile snow of Spring
In the still light of my heart
        I sing to you:
Not for the struttings of the barnyard bird
Nor the clanging of his woe,
        Scattering the piebald snow;
Not for the wrappings of the grasping hen
Nor the stressing of her region
        To a one-leggèd reason,
                As the pyeing snow,
                Coloring to the green,
                Becomes obscene . . .
Where is the way of it?
Where is the way
        To the heart—the heart!
I cannot find the clock of Time.
I cannot touch the hands of day.
        Your hands! Your hands
                Point the way of it,
                Point the way
                To the heart—the heart.

The snow fails and the birds to the North,
White in their flight with the skying Spring;
But yet, in the still light of my heart,
With the futile snow — to you I sing.

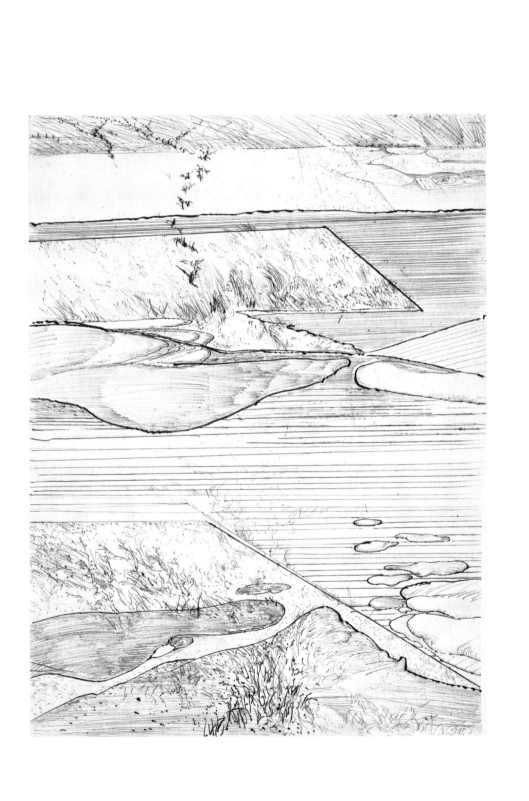

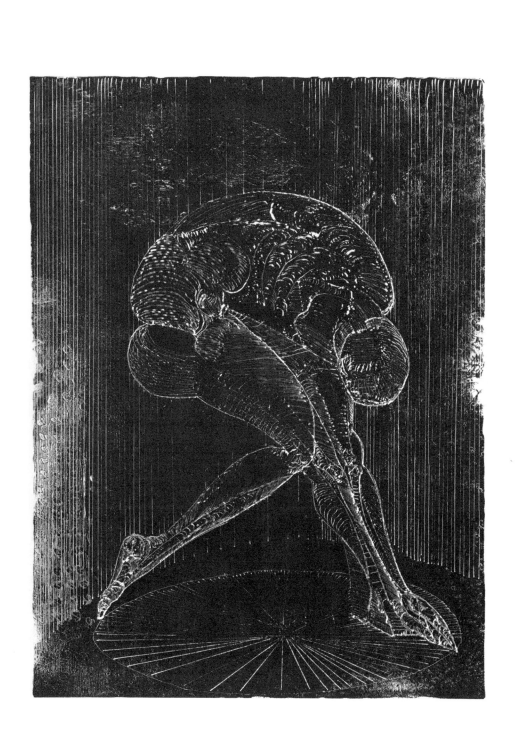

WHEN I HAVE GATHERED-IN THE NIGHT

Who can time the clocking hours,
Who can time where day begins
When I have gathered-in the night;
When I have stalked from space to space
In all compartments of my heart.
Who can time the clocking hours,
Who can tell the tolling time
In all the rooms where I reside
And lie myself to sleep at night,
And lie myself to sleep at night
In all compartments of my heart.

When loss is in the night and darkness glooms the day,
The hours drag me by: the years would fly away;
The sea brings in the night and deep receiving me
Again, again, I turn, to the anchoring sea . . .

Blear to the night
On into obsoleting night
Buoyed past jetties
Past the shale; dark of the night.
Blear, blear to the heart
Heeled to the wind
With no answering helm
Striven past silence
Past the shoals; time of the night.
On: on: in obsoleting night . . .

SEA CHANTEY

Aleatory wind on the numinous sea,
The wail of the harkness is in the sail!
Gust to a time when I was free,
Aleatory wind on the numinous sea;

The sail is luffing — no one to hail —
Listing to starb'rd — though helm's-a'-lee —
Caught here in irons — three steps to bail —
Yet the wail of the harkness is in the sail!

O aleatory wind of a numinous sea . . .

SONNET

Primitive, in my perpetual dawn,
I seek the sea edged by a sundry sky;
And flail watered notions that tyrannize
And monstrous bankrupt the lovelier word.

Give way of theories — they destroy the wise:
Accede back through the eloquent heart;
Give in to the clouds and the awesome day,
Curl in the sea at the edge of the sky

While tedious license stifles the past
(Ignoring music that inures the heart,
Ignoring mere language — seamster of thought);
Let the freer declaim! Mediocre
On the trolling sea drained of denizen
Primitive to my perpetual dawn.

You! who have startled
    the sound of the sea,
You! who are startled—
    startled like me,
Give to the time—
    the time of the sea,
And walk in the marsh—
    the marsh of the sea . . .

Erinna lived in the southeastern Aegean and probably wrote during the fourth century B.C. The ancients regarded the nineteen-year-old as second only to Sappho among women poets. Fragments of the poem were discovered in 1928.

ERINNA TO BAUCIS

. . . Deep into the wave you raced,
Leaping from white horses,
Whirling the night on running feet.
But loudly I shouted, "Dearest,
You're mine!" Then you, the Tortoise,
Skipping, ran to the rutted garth
Of the great court. These things I
Lament and sorrow, sad Baucis.
These are for me, O Maiden,
Warm trails back through my heart:
Joy, once filled, smoulders in ash;
Young, in rooms without a care,
We held our miming dolls—girls
In the pretense of young brides
(And the toward-dawn-mother
Lotted wool to tending women,
Calling Baucis to salt the meat);
O, what trembling when we were small
And fear was brought by MORMO—

Huge of ear up on her head,
With four feet walking, always
Changing from face to other.

But mounted in the bed of
Your husband, dearest Baucis,
You forgot things heard from mother,
While still the littler child.
Fast Aphrodite set your
Forgetful heart. So I lament,
Neglecting though your obsequies:
Unprofaned, my feet may not leave
And my naked hair's not loosed abroad,
No lighted eye may disgrace your corpse
And in this house, O my Baucis,
Purpling shame grips me about.
Wretched Erinna! Nineteen,
I moan with a blush to grieve. . . .
Old women voice the mortal bloom. . . .
One cries out the lamenting flame. . . .
Hymen! . . . O Hymenaeus! . . .
While the night whirls unvoiced
Darkness is on my eyes . . .

Antipater, who wrote during the second century B.C.,
lived in the city of Sidon in Phoenicia.

ANTIPATER OF SIDON ON ERINNA

Erinna's words are few — no excess in her song,
Her little epic chanced the lotting of the Muse;
For her remembrance — no music ceased away
Or black in the bind of night's shadowy wing.

Yet we, the countless fashioned throng of poets,
Lie rotting, Stranger — battalioned in forgetfulness:
The croaking jackdaws scattered in the springtime clouds
Are as nothing to the soft murmurs of the swan.

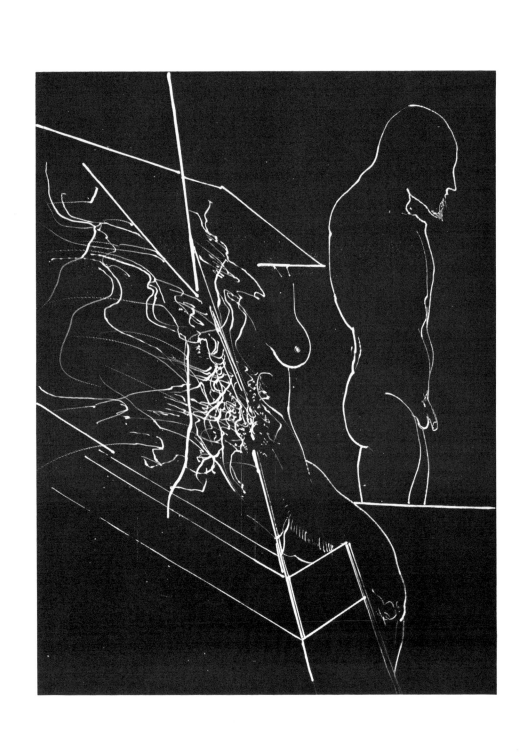

Archilochus, a wandering mercenary from the island of Paros in the south Aegean whose name means "first sergeant," wrote during the eighth or seventh century B.C. This poem, discovered in 1964, is his longest extant fragment.

ARCHILOCHUS SEDUCING

. . ."Contain yourself! I, too, endure!
  Ah, calm yourself—although,
  If hurried, and the spirit goads,
  There is a waiting virgin here,
  Gentle of the lovelier strain;
  Soft with desire—she'd marry now . . .
  Indeed, her sorrows are for you
  Though faultless do I find her form."

Then I countered things she'd said:
"O daughter of Amphimedo
(Now remembered—noble and wise—
There in the bind of darkening earth),
The ample goddess brings delights
Apart from the divine affair;
Of these, young men may be sufficed . . .
Let's council with the willing gods
And, when all the shadows blacken,
At our leisure, take our pleasure;
Though, as you order, I'll abide!

"I've known to wait with my desire,
Beneath the arch—beside the gate . . .
Ah, don't begrudge my course, dear friend,
I'm for the garden bearing grass.

"Now Neobulé's forgotten!
She is—alas!—just overripe,
Another man may have her—fallen
Long since from the tree of her bloom
And the charm that she'd had before;
Raving in lust of satiety
This harridan flaunts her vigor...
To the crows with her! The neighbor's
Laugh won't be on a wife of mine!

"Ah, it is you I wish—neither
Dishonest nor other-sided;
While she is quick with anger
And many are her friends—urged
Toward eagerness, I fear
Lest the get, as from a throwing bitch,
Drop blind—and on the wrong day!"

Saying so, I reached for the girl:
Among a burst of flowers
Gently she's prone—then placing
Her neck to my pillowed-arm,
We hid within my tender cloak . . .
Tremble-eyed, as a fawn with fear,
Her breasts were encouraged; so sweet
My hand caressed—then I revealed
My raw skin ever-new; entertained
With intruded vigor: and gaining
The whole beauty of her body
Let loose the white force of my strength
As lightly I touched her yellow hair.

Lentulus Gaetulicus, a Roman consul who wrote during the first century A.D., was executed by the Emperor Gaius.

GAETULICUS' EPITAPH ON ARCHILOCHUS

Here, by-the-sea, is the sign of his tomb:
Archilochus! who bloodied civil Helicon
When he immersed a bitter Muse, first
With the viperous venom of his wrath;

O wayfarer, pass softly by, indeed:
Lest rouse the settled wasps of his lone sleep;
Flowing with tears, the keening Lycambes
Has known the sting—three daughters hanged
                                    themselves.

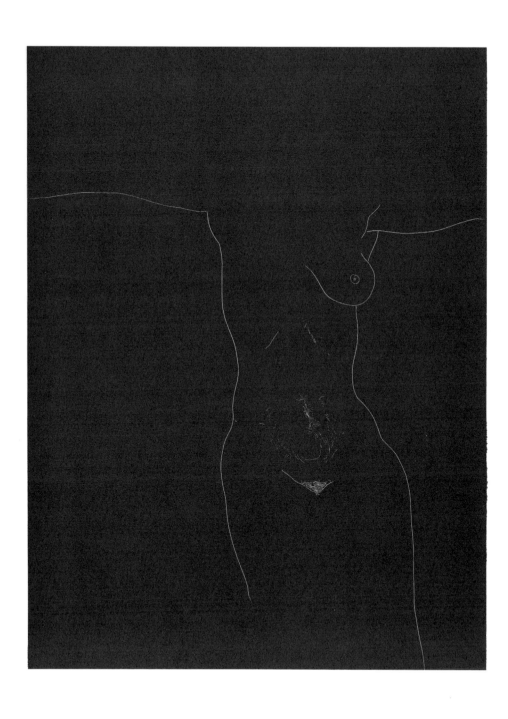

Praxilla, who wrote during the fifth century B.C., lived
in the city of Sicyon, near Corinth.
These five fragments comprise her extant work.

PRAXILLA CONVERSING

HE: O preening glance—latticing down!
     You've the face of a nymph,
     Though woman below. . . .

SHE: Gird for the rock, O companion,
      And the scorpion under. . . .

HE: Remember the words of Admetus:
     Give way of evil man and men;
     They bring, we learn, the small delight.
     O companion!—of good men, love. . . .

SHE: Of the lovelier things I leave behind
      Are the gleams of the sun,
      Then the face of the moon
      And the sheen of the stars—
      Yet cucumbers ripen with apples and pears. . . .

HE: Though in your breast, like Achilles,
     Your soul is never persuaded . . .

29

Zenobius, who lived in the second century A.D., was a
collector and compiler of ancient proverbs.

AFTER ZENOBIUS ON PRAXILLA

For those who say that "sillier" is her and her Adonis,
I'd say this Sicyonian was quite a lyric poet
(Ah, that is Polemon's accord); but she, herself, Praxilla,
Has raised—alas!—a question: why are the lovelier thing.
Exchanged for vegetables? O, may one but juxtapose,
To the cucumber at best, the celestial firmament?

Perhaps Praxilla's silly, just a foolish simpleton;
Or is she unselfconscious, as we all might wish to be?
(Indeed, the root of cucumber cognates with Sicyon,
And lest I mention phallic—and is that now obvious?)
Tho' all of the new critics would have probably compared
The cucumber that ripens with the apple and the pear.

MIDNIGHT. AND A RAMBLING SKY

Lady, I cannot say I'm pleased with me
As I pare the gap of age and youth,
And I wander in the wait of night
And I wonder where the wrong began;

Lady, if we could now just have met
And Time were back to younger time . . .
But Love defaults to a rambling sky:
The stars lean down and quietly laugh.

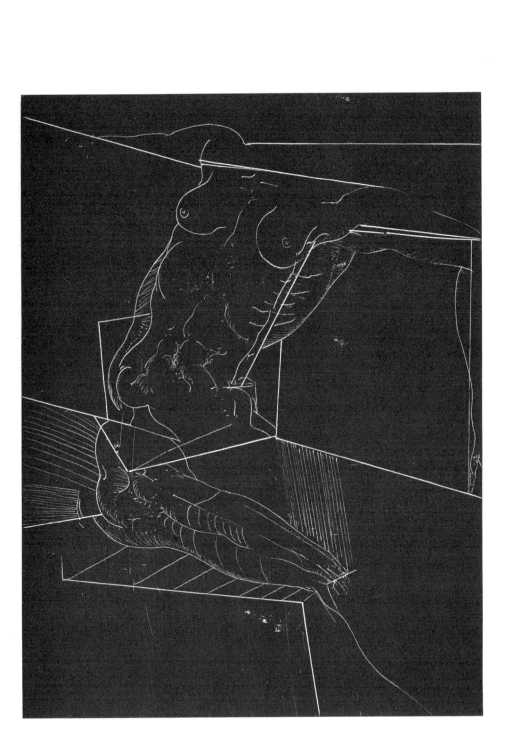

EARLY OF AN EVENING

In the early of the evening,
    While the world was marking time,
She left without a reason,
    And yet with some alarm;

Her thoughts were all of going,
    She wouldn't seem to stay
In the early of the evening,
    While the world was marking time.

SONNET

A letter from the Virgin Isles

"When you have resolved what it is you want,
And can think of me in the tender time;
Then I'll come to you (in the tender time)
— Hold trembling hand to a trembling hand.

But now you live in another's house,
And walk with him (in another's house),
Yet cling to me with a trembling hand
And surprise a fierceness of my heart!

Give up this thought — leave me be — Love, I say,
Is a catholic thing: affairs are not
By Love construed as other than the world
Has known. Conduct your way! Compose yourself!
Woman, I say: don't come when Time is terse!"
He keeps the woman, while I hold the verse.

THE JOURNEYING GIRL

Go ramble in the lolling hills,
Yet stay with me this gruffing night;
You neighbored Love, O journeying girl,
In the fretted surface of the day.

DIRGE IN FLIGHT

Yet astride the peccant moon,
Sad sail pillowing to the sky,
Perceptive on the spread of night;
Too long we flutter in the bind.

Imperious bird declaims the dawn,
Then deigns a step from out the sky...
I remember! I remember!
Night of the moon may descend to a bird
Whose perch preludes the freeze of vanity:
Pride's pejoration for the trenchant day.

I suppose, of course, nothing's new
    [. . . though flowers are few
    in the heart of the world!]
Except, of course, my love for her;

And though, of course, we are but two
    [. . . she severed and strew
    in the heart of my world!]
I would have been but one with her.

AUBADE

No child of morning

Let us say I'm sad for all the world.
Oh, let's just say I'm sad for me and you:
 You cannot change the things you do
 And I—no child of morning,
 Though yet of yesterday—
 I cannot stay!
Let us say I'm silent to the world.
Oh, let's just say I'm silently unfurled
 While whispering up a spiral
 And revealed—I cannot change
 The hum of you and me—
 It is easy
As the hero; hard to live a life . . .
Oh, let's just say I'm sad for all the world.

IN THE WAIT OF NIGHT

I, by-a-lake, face a scouring sky
And think of the time when Love lay by,
                    My love lay by:
Delightedly eating — wine we were drinking,
When I and my love faced the scouring sky,
                    The scouring sky;
Now, I, on my back, with a book to delight,
Think of hours to come in the wait of night,
                    The wait of night:
Listlessly dreaming and noteworthy seeming,
I'll think of the time when Love lay by,
                    My love lay by.

A TALE

Although he knew it to be insane, the truth was known. He stood bowed and observing; his hurts were his character, and that his destiny. Preceding himself with naïveté, he had suited in arrogance of the unarmed and waited. She came. The wrong woman. He wanted her and they traveled, the moon being lit in the mouth of the sky. Imaging him, she was weakest of the strong and strongest of the weak. She was as the face of the moon; he the gleaming of the sun. No. She was the sun and he the other—pallid alternation. Dybbuks danced on a frosted cake, bouquets of laughter lined the aisle; as he was strewn about, memories crowded the jewel box of his soul . . . he prepared to place grief's mantle on: the truth was known and he knew it to be insane.

BALLAD

Kiss the hills for me—just once

In the night of my heart
I cannot think—in the dark time
Where you are—or who you're with
But your heart's alone—I know
Alone in the dark time!

Kiss the hills for me—just once
Then sigh with the breeze—just once
Relate to the trees—as once
We laughed at the seas
Though now you grieve me!

In the night of my heart
Tears freeze from my cheek
The cheek that you touched
Touched in the dark time!
I stand near the house
And look to the wild
From the home you won't keep
From the home you won't keep
What do you want—searching for might
What do you want—alone with the night
O what do you want—alone—I know
Alone in the dark time!

Kiss the hills for me—just once
Then sigh with the breeze—just once
Relate to the trees—as once
We laughed at the seas
Though now you grieve me!

In the night of your heart
Would you think—in the dark time
   Oh, no!
Won't intrude in your schemes
   Oh, no!
You're young with Fame—it seems
An only woman now
Searching for might—what do you want
Alone with the night—what do you want
O what do you want—alone—I know
Alone in the dark time!

Kiss the hills for me—just once
Then sigh with the breeze—just once
Relate to the trees—as once
We laughed at the seas
Though now you leave me!

SONG OF THE UNWARY OAF

Little flower — of twisted root
How dare you play a singing lute?

Won't you know — the day's not right
To dance and sing in Michal's sight?

Stubborn flower — why rise to grow
Struggling soil is teemed below

O little flower — bend your head
Give in! Give in! Enough to shed

The little flower — unwary oaf
Stubborn, stiff-necked, foolish growth

Laughed and played his singing lute:
"Twisted is a changeling word
How it's used is surely moot!"

BLINKING BUOY

Let the staunchness of the night defend!
 I'll have no wives—or other lives
Caught between two days that blend,
Searing the time when I offend

The looming moon on the pinioned sky;
 I'll have no wives—or other lives!
But the coasted harbor gleamed a sigh
As the gloating buoy blinks me by.

Beat to quarters! Here creatives' rant!
 I'll have no ties—or other lies:
Hear the cadence of commercial cant
Culling jargon for the sycophant;

The carrying sound of the heaving wave
    (I'll have no ties—or other lies)
Rushes on by and I am still, save
The disquiet of a quiet grave;

And the coasted harbor gleams a sigh,
And the carrying sound rushed on by;

Gloats the blinking buoy as I fend . . .

DAWN IN LATTER AUGUST

Morning streams path tides of day,
Closing flowers hide their sheen,
Stretching women search policy;
And sullen summer sleeps away...

No man can walk abroad save on his own shadow

Sir Walter Raleigh

ibi semper omne vitae spatium famula fuit. CATULLUS

ATTIS

Mad—with the moon—on the Phrygian shore
He danced as the night—the night which spread
He wound in the night—and ecstasy fed
And ecstasy grew—and the tendrils bled
Though in his heart—his heart now dead
The dance had ceased—only night was spread!

FRANZ KAFKA

Round my head—through a broken door
Weaving there—while I beg for more
Round and round—the listening night
Crawling me—with a biting blight
Roaches inveigh—the waiting floor
No more—no more—Gregor...

"I am suspected of something—it is in the air. There is something behind me."
VINCENT VAN GOGH to his brother Theo, while begging him not to
name the baby 'Vincent.' (They had a dead older brother named
Vincent; and when Theo's baby was so named, the painter had
himself committed.)

VINCENT VAN GOGH

Madman Vincent! — why dare to dare?
An emetic battle couldn't be won
The other Vincent was always there
But not living Esau — to be outcharmed
And I would say I agree with you
Another Vincent was cause for alarm!

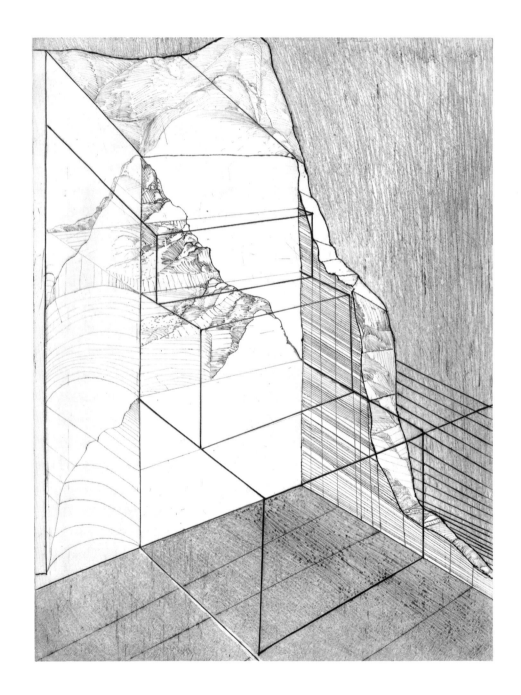

WILLIAM SHAKESPEARE

Splicing Sonnet LXIV

When I have seen the hungry ocean gain
Advantage on the kingdom of the shore,
And the firm soil win from watery main—
Increasing store with loss and loss with store;

When I have seen such interchange of state,
Or state itself confounded to decay,
Ruin has taught me how to ruminate—
Time will come and take my love away.

EDWARD DAHLBERG

Edward died — will no one grieve
Chided friends — will you believe
He'd stroke the heart — don't turn away!
Chided friends — will you allow
Little lamb — who made you growl?

Edward died — will no one grieve
Daughters of Saul — will you perceive
What lady would deny a heat
When Edward danced the saline street
Little lamb — who made you growl?

Edward died — will no one grieve
O lady barber — will you receive
Squatting in the alley wet
Concupiscent thoughts are met
Little lamb — who made you growl?

Edward died—will no one grieve
Chided friends—will you believe
He'd stroke the heart—don't be dismayed
Chided friends—O please allow!
Little lamb—who made you growl?

Though Perdix's uncle, Daedalus, falsely pretended that Perdix had fallen by accident, he was banished from Athens for his nephew's death: Minerva, pitying the twelve-year-old who was a greater carpenter than his uncle, changed Perdix into the first partridge; and Daedalus sailed to Crete with his young son Icarus.

PERDIX

From misprision I would fly
I made the saw and compass
And yet—I fear a height
Perdix!—then Icarus!

If not so very far
A partridge still may ply
I think I shall decide
Just how high is high . . .

Daniel da Volterra was commissioned by the Vatican to paint cloths
over the genitalia of Michelangelo's male figures on
"The Last Judgment." He became known as *Braghettone*.

GIOVANNI ANGELO MEDICI

It was Pius the Fourth
Who ordered a cloth!
And had breeches adorn,
So he wouldn't fawn;
And no longer giggle,
At nudes by Michel-
Angelo!

He mauled them everyone without mercy. It was easy enough to see he was an author! ALAIN RENÉ LE SAGE

THE POETASTER

"Not without lessons! —you're writing a verse?
Come loiter on my euphonious perch
Twelve dollars the hour—unmetered fee
Often the *Village Voice* has published me!"

But reduce no Human Spirit to Disgrace of Price. EMILY DICKINSON

SOLILOQUY WITHIN A TELEPHONE CALL

"What! —you've sold my painting?
A buyer will come? —it cannot be!"

Was no monetary deal! —a painting for a poem
You suggested we exchange! —a painting for a poem
You seemed to need my poem—near you while at work
Surely I would gain—a transfer such as this
You said it wasn't money—we shared a carrion sea
And the painting seemed to grow—a pushy kind of art
Commanded by the colors to stop and look at them
I couldn't help but yield to the painting on the wall

"What! —I had my chance? —you've kept the poem?
I may borrow another? —ah—my friend!"

Too shrewd for me—indeed—Dahlberg was right:
People don't change—they only stand more revealed
Ah—my friend—the bond was of other issue when
I couldn't help but yield to the painting on the wall

The study of the beautiful is a duel in which the artist cries out with fear before he is vanquished. CHARLES BAUDELAIRE

ARTISTS DINING IN THE HAMPTONS

"Then you're giving a dinner? — not without me! —
To improve my Art — I'll leave a husband home —
And improve cachet — with a gallery-drone —
Then delight in my canvas!" — [that vanquished me] —

REFRAIN

When young—with opening desire
A closure they'd provide
Now I crouch rather low
And do my best to hide . . .

TO AN OLD FRIEND

On a whorl spindling
   in the swirl of the world,
You are no friend!
The straw man nailed
   to yet another cross
Invites the anguish
   of other loss,
And the emulous-plan
   to resurrect the sin
Begins again — and again begins;
Perched in the place
   of your unseeing eyes,
I am not as you think
And you are no friend!

THE TROUT DUET

Trout? — don't look at me like that!
You thought the fly was real —
Don't look at me like that!
Oh, easy as the ethical trout
While wriggling on a line —
Ideas of ordered Nature
Were different swimming free —
(Some cooling water as we chat, Trout?)
O Trout! — my problem's not with you —
Nor even with the fly —
It truly runs to pleasure —
Liar that I am — Trout!
Don't condescend to scan
My sybaritic soul —
I'd rather sit this rock
And think your murderous swims
Than sight that side to me —
Trout? — don't look at me like that!
Be sanctimonious with a minnow —
Trout!

SEVEN BY NIGHT

1

The exaggerating moon
lit the tree of night
slow in the silence . . .

2

The febrile moon of night
descends the sky
beguiled by proud flesh . . .

3

The flouting moon
comes to the bed of truth
stunned the silence festers . . .

4

Somber timbrel in the night
repel the song
of an audacious moon . . .

5

Cityward then
pliant night accedes
into the ganging of the day...

6

Thronging to the day
city-wealth accumulates
men decay...

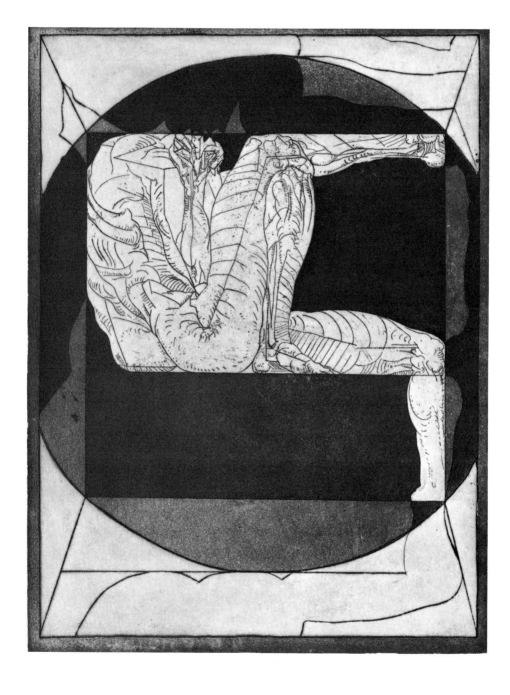

7

Exalting the day
of the unmooned night
now anthropophobic man . . .

Walk with me.
Where the moon is slung
In incising night,
Walk with me and hold my hand . . .

SONNET

Let Time, in disparagement of days,
Inure the soul that yearns to accede,
Through regions of loss and little praise:

Where jackdaws winging caw the sky
And stult the cuddings of the blest
(The easy ones are blessed, they say,
Not caught between two days, they say);
Where nighttime grackles wander wide
And strut with pleasures their behest;
Birching sentinels arch unaware
As enrageous claims define the field . . .
Bold shrubs align this blurting sphere!

O Time, who loafs to lose one's self,
How different is the discourse of today?

Bleak of the heart and hearth
I recollect myself
In the gnaw of January;
A little movement, so far
On the crippling snow . . .

And in conjunction with a day,
Slow dreams are dreamt in ripen'd Time,
Though shadows bleaken in reproach
When in conjunction with a day;

And in conjunction with a day,
As dear again as dear to me,
How sad a thing is sadness now
When in conjunction with a day.

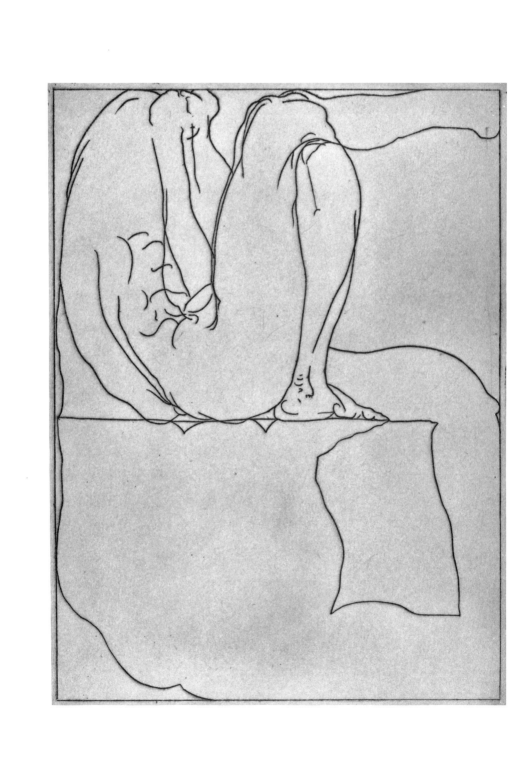

In a fantasy of my wilder heart,
As deafened silence loots the night,
        Yes, loots the night!
Edged to extremity while all's asleep,
        Yes, all asleep!
If the angry night would only weep,
        Only weep . . . .
As squall clouds bloat the quickened sky
Ruminations rain on the ruined dawn
Again I ask: and again ask why

In a sea-dreamed cloister-house,
Lived by the walls of the night,
Lived with the fear of a fear
    And the turf-side clashings;

In a sea-dreamed cloister-house,
Lived of a Time dismembered,
Lived with the old sea lashings
    And no one to answer;

In a sea-dreamed cloister-house,
Lived; — though the night remembers
And unruffled flows the sky
    Above the draggled beach . . .

In the inchoate plan we do not define,
Stumbling past the placid rock,
Loathly reeling in aggressive shade —
Now the rising beauty of a terrible moon . . .

BIRD IN FLIGHT

Dear little bird!
Flown from the wildings of her hair
As a gift of Time that wends,
Glisk with delight a gentler song.
In the drift of Time the way begins
And Time unfolds and Time descends.

Dear little bird!
So zealous in refulgence:
Lilting streams and tumbling voids,
Drenching rocks — soon pleat the night.
In the drift of Time the way begins
And Time unfolds and Time descends.

Dear little bird?
Why disquieted, though tempted?
Why, arrogated to dismay?
With lamentation, look and pass! . . .
In the drift of Time the way begins
And Time unfolds and Time descends.

Dear little bird!
Free solitary. Spirit alone.
Unbound probate, homeless on the earth,
Fly, O fly: on wings of weakness — fly!
Frail Jeremiah. Probate of Time.
    Dear little bird . . .
Time unfolds and Time descends,
In the drift of Time the way begins
And Time unfolds and Time descends.

AFTERWORD

There is a certain sycamore tree
Down by old Hillary Brook,
Come wander to the sycamore tree,
But bring the doubts I took;

You'll find the way is easy,
Though a path's been lost some nights,
Just ask the one who answers
The source of Hillary Brook . . .

A NOTE ON THE POET & PAINTER & TYPE

Daniel Haberman's previous book, POEMS, was published by Art Direction Book Company in 1977. Born in New York City in 1933, he attended the Walden School, Carnegie-Mellon University and the graduate school of New York University. He was educated in the secondhand book shops of Manhattan, and by two years of study with Edward Dahlberg. He is the designer of this book.

Jan Stussy's paintings are permanently owned by museums and public and private collections in this country and abroad. He has also won an Academy Award for his film documentary of a quadriplegic painter. Born in Benton County, Missouri in 1921, he is Professor (6) of Painting at UCLA.

The typeface Cochin is an adaptation of a type design of French descent. Both the Roman and Italic are based on copperplate engraved lettering made by the eighteenth-century painter and engraver, Charles Nicolas Cochin. The letters were generally associated with the descriptions of pictures and also appeared on the frames of portraits. The work of Cochin exerted considerable influence in bringing about decorative type and ornamental letters.